Lourdes Diary

Other Loyola Press Books by James Martin, SJ

My Life with the Saints

Awake My Soul: Contemporary Catholics on Traditional Devotions (editor)

Celebrating Good Liturgy: A Guide to the Ministries of the Massn (editor)

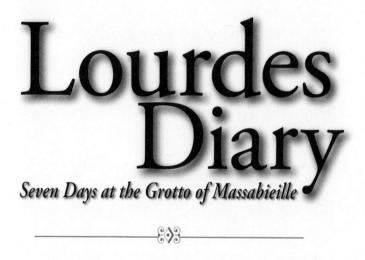

Lourdes Diary

Seven Days at the Grotto of Massabieille

JAMES MARTIN, SJ

LOYOLAPRESS.

CHICAGO

LOYOLAPRESS.

3441 N. ASHLAND AVENUE
CHICAGO, ILLINOIS 60657
(800) 621-1008
WWW.LOYOLABOOKS.ORG

Cover photo by Burns McLindon
Cover design by Mia Basile
Interior design by Kathryn Seckman Kirsch

Library of Congress Cataloging-in-Publication Data
Martin, James, S.J.
  Lourdes diary : seven days at the Grotto of Massabieille / James Martin.
     p. cm.
  Includes bibliographical references.
  ISBN-13: 978-0-8294-2397-6
  ISBN-10: 0-8294-2397-4
  1. Mary, Blessed Virgin, Saint—Apparitions and miracles—France—Lourdes.
2. Christian pilgrims and pilgrimages—France—Lourdes. 3. Christian
shrines—France—Lourdes. 4. Lourdes (France)—Religious life and customs.
5. Bernadette, Saint, 1844–1879. 6. Martin, James, S.J. 7. Lourdes (France)—
Church history. I. Title.
BT653.M3485 2006
232.91'7094478—dc22

                                                                2006004929

Printed in the United States of America
06 07 08 09 10 Versa 10 9 8 7 6 5 4 3 2 1

For the members and friends of the Order of Malta, in
gratitude for their generosity, companionship,
and example.

Apart from the apparitions, nothing before or after singled her out for special notice. There are only traces in the stories of her interactions and a few letters indicating the strength of her personality and the particularity of her spirituality, but in these residues Bernadette begins to reveal herself to us.

RUTH HARRIS, *LOURDES: BODY AND SPIRIT IN THE SECULAR AGE*

I have told the events. Let people abide by what I said the first time. I may have forgotten and so may others. The simpler one writes, the better it will be.

BERNADETTE SOUBIROUS, APRIL 7, 1879

❧CONTENTS☙

A Life with the Saints

During my second year as a Jesuit novice, I wandered into the community television room one Friday evening to see what video was being served up. Television watching was a popular pastime for novices living on a thirty-five-dollar monthly stipend in our novitiate, located in a poor neighborhood in Boston, Massachusetts.

In typical Jesuit style, our TV room consisted of fifteen individual recliners lined up in front of a large television, an admittedly strange setup that once prompted my brother-in-law to ask if, besides vows of poverty, chastity, and obedience, we took a vow against sofas, too.

"What's on?" I asked the other novices as I walked into the TV room.

"*The Song of Bernadette,*" said one, glancing up from the TV.

"What's it about?" I asked.

Everyone looked up from his recliner, apparently aghast.

"You're kidding, right?" said another novice. "Please tell me you're kidding."

I shook my head dumbly.

One thing I realized soon after joining the Jesuits was how little Catholic culture I had grown up with, or at least absorbed. Though both my parents were good Catholics, our family lived in a predominantly Jewish neighborhood where bar mitzvahs were more common than first Holy Communion parties. My sister and I attended public schools, and the two of us darkened the doors of the parish church only on Sundays and holy days of obligation.

As a boy, then, I was about as likely to join something like the Catholic Youth Organization or become an altar server as I was to join the circus. Cub Scouts, which most of my school friends belonged to, and where we carved miniature racing cars for the Pinewood Derby in September, sliced up pumpkins and made papier-mâché masks in October, made bows and arrows in November, fashioned construction-paper chains for Christmas trees in December, and learned about the local "Indian" lore for the rest of the year, seemed far more interesting than being an altar boy. As far as I knew, altar servers didn't get to make their own arrowheads.

Later on, as an undergraduate at the University of Pennsylvania, I was given ample opportunities and several invitations to join the active Newman Club on campus. That organization, named after the English Catholic convert (and later cardinal) John Henry Newman, was founded to nourish the spiritual lives of Catholic students at non-Catholic universities. For thousands of undergraduates, it is an easy way to connect with other like-minded Catholics. (Just recently, I found out that the Newman Club was actually founded at Penn, in 1893.)

But I was more than satisfied with the local parish church, which I attended on (most) Sundays, and I turned up my nose at the Newman Club, since I harbored suspicions that anyone who joined must be some sort of "fanatic." Thus another excellent opportunity to learn more about my faith was passed by.

A few years ago, as a Jesuit, I returned to Penn to give a brief talk on my vocation journey to, of all groups, graduate students at the Wharton School of Business. One person in the audience asked how often I went to the Newman Club as an undergraduate. Embarrassed, I had to admit, "Never."

So while the other Jesuits in my novitiate had been raised in families that went to daily Mass, attended novenas, said grace at meals, and knew the difference between the Immaculate Heart and the Sacred Heart, I was still trying to remember how many sacraments there were.

And while the other novices had attended Catholic grammar schools, high schools, and even colleges, and had studied church history, systematic theology, moral theology, and both Testaments, I was still trying to figure out why confession was now called the sacrament of reconciliation.

Needless to say, I had a lot to learn during the novitiate.

Sometimes I was amazed that the Jesuits had even accepted me. The assistant novice director once asked me, "Are you sure you're Catholic?"

My ignorance extended not only to weighty theological matters but also to pop culture. In the space of a few months in the novitiate, I had already been teased mercilessly by the other novices for not having seen *Going My Way, The Nun's*

Story, and *The Trouble with Angels.* Now I didn't know *The Song of Bernadette.* I feared that this was another instance of me not knowing a movie that everyone else had seen by age ten.

"Sit down," one of the novices said. "You can't say you're Catholic and not have seen this movie."

Based on Franz Werfel's best-selling novel of the same name, *The Song of Bernadette* tells the story of the events that occurred in the small French town of Lourdes during the latter part of the nineteenth century. The movie, starring Jennifer Jones as Bernadette and Charles Bickford as her initially doubtful but eventually supportive pastor, has become a perennial Catholic favorite. It was my first introduction to one of the great saints of modern times, a person who has become a model for me in my own life.

At the time, I had little of what one might call a "devotion" to any saint, let alone St. Bernadette. As a boy, I had prayed assiduously before a plastic statue of St. Jude, patron of hopeless causes, who stood atop a dresser in my bedroom. Over the years, I suppose, he put in a good word for me when I wanted to pass a spelling test or do well in Little

League tryouts. But later on, I began to see prayer to the saints as somewhat superstitious and even ridiculous.

As a Jesuit novice, however, I was introduced to a new way of seeing the saints: as human beings whose lives I could use as models for my own. This was how my fellow Jesuits approached the saints, not simply as distant heavenly figures upon whom one called for divine favors, but as fellow Christians.

In her marvelous book *Friends of God and Prophets,* the theologian Elizabeth Johnson speaks of two primary models of the saints: patrons and companions.

Probably the more common model today is the saint as *patron,* the intercessor who pleads on our behalf before God. This was the model I was using (without knowing it, of course) as I prayed before the statue of St. Jude in my bedroom as a child. As a novice, I was introduced to the second model: the saint as *companion*—in other words, as one who accompanies us in our lives as Christians, who teaches us how to follow Jesus Christ, and who shows us new ways to be holy.

For me, the most satisfying part of seeing the saints as companions was realizing how different they were, leading lives that often seemed quite the opposite of one another.

Thomas Aquinas, the thirteenth-century theologian, for instance, had dozens of books on hand for his studies, while the poverty-minded Francis of Assisi told his Franciscans never to own even *one,* lest they become too proud. (If a man has a book, said Francis, then he'll want a shelf, then a library, and finally someone to bring him his books from his library.) On his road to sanctity, Ignatius of Loyola gave up a soldiering career, while Joan of Arc began one. The French Carmelite nun Thérèse of Lisieux lived within the walls of a cloistered monastery and had little contact with the outside world, while the great Jesuit missionary Francis Xavier traveled to Africa, India, and Japan to spread the gospel.

The saints are not carbon copies of one another.

Each of the saints shows us what it means to be holy in *this* particular way, as Karl Rahner, the Jesuit theologian, has written. We are meant to follow the path to sanctity in our own way. "For me to be a saint means to be myself," the Trappist Thomas Merton wrote.

These days I see the saints as *both* patrons and companions. Through their examples, they help me lead a Christian life and trust that God calls me to sanctity through my own life, in my own unique circumstances, and in my own way. And I believe that through their prayers, they help me be a better Christian. So: patrons and companions.

But I knew none of this when I sat down in the novitiate that night to watch *The Song of Bernadette*. And I certainly knew nothing of the story of Bernadette Soubirous and what happened to her at Lourdes. Yet as moving as the film is, the real story—the story of the young woman who would become a saint, and would become for me a patron and companion—is even more so.

2

The Story of a Soul

In 1858, Bernadette Soubirous, age fourteen, was living in appalling poverty in a small town in southern France. Her father's milling business had failed, and, desperate for lodgings, the family took up residence in a room that until recently had served as the local jail. (Today it is still called the *cachot,* the French word for "jail" or "dungeon.") In this cramped hovel, no more than ten by ten feet square, lived Bernadette's parents and their four children. The first few pages of Franz Werfel's novel capture what must have been the misery of Bernadette's parents, particularly her once-proud father: "What annoys him more than this wretched room is the two barred windows, one larger, one smaller, these two abject squinting eyes turned on the filthy yard of the Cachot where the dunghill of the whole neighborhood stinks to heaven."

On February 11, Bernadette went with her sister, Toinette, and a friend to fetch some firewood—the family's poverty prevented Bernadette's mother from buying wood in the town. Only a few months prior, Bernadette had returned to her family after working as a shepherdess in a nearby town to earn a little money.

The girls' destination was a grotto on the outskirts of Lourdes at a place called Massabieille (the name means "old rock" in the local patois), on the banks of the fast-flowing Gave River. In her superb study of Bernadette's apparitions and their consequences, *Lourdes: Body and Spirit in the Secular Age,* the Oxford historian Ruth Harris reminds readers of the unappealing state of the now-famous grotto. From as early as the seventeenth century, the town's pigs had come to forage at Massabieille, and they eventually took up residence there. Far from the well-tended and even manicured setting that contemporary pilgrims know, the original site, says Harris, was "a marginal and even filthy place."

While the two other girls crossed the river to gather wood from the opposite bank, Bernadette, a sickly and asthmatic child, lingered. Eventually, she began to remove her stockings, to prepare to wade into the river and join them. As she did so, she heard the sound of a wind, though she saw nothing moving around her. Bending down to remove her other stocking, she looked up again.

This time, the wind swayed a small rosebush in the niche of the grotto, and a "gentle light" emanated from the spot. Bernadette later reported seeing a young girl in that light, dressed in white, smiling at her. (Later interpretations of Bernadette's testimony, including those in *The Song of Bernadette,* misrepresent the vision as a mature woman.)

Frightened, Bernadette took a rosary from her pocket and tried to make the sign of the cross. Fear got the better of her, and she found herself unable to do so. But when the young girl made the sign of the cross, Bernadette did the same, and began to pray.

Here is the description of what happened in Bernadette's own words:

> The vision made the Sign of the Cross. Then I tried a second time, and I could. As soon as I made the Sign of the Cross, the fearful shock I felt disappeared. I

knelt down and I said my rosary in the presence
of the beautiful lady. The vision fingered the beads
of her own rosary, but she did not move her lips.
When I finished my rosary, she signed for me to
approach; but I did not dare. Then she disappeared,
just like that.

This would be the first of several apparitions that Bernadette
reported. At that first apparition and all the rest, no one
with her heard, saw, or experienced anything.

On the way home, Bernadette told her sister what she
had seen, swearing her to secrecy. But upon entering their
house, Toinette burst out with the news to her mother:
"Bernadette saw a white girl in the Grotto of Massabieille!"
Her parents, furious at Bernadette's apparent lies, beat her
and forbade her to return.

A few days later, still confused about what had happened at Massabieille, Bernadette told a local priest in the
confessional about her vision. Astonished by her compo-
sure and the clarity with which she related the story, he
asked her permission to speak of it to the pastor, Abbé
Dominique Peyramale. According to the exhaustive

biography *Bernadette of Lourdes,* written by the French historian René Laurentin in 1979, all that Peyramale had to say was "We must wait and see."

Neighbors and friends tried to convince Bernadette's parents to change their minds about not letting Bernadette return to the grotto. One town notable told her father, sensibly, "A lady with a rosary—that can't be anything bad." Eventually her parents relented, and Bernadette returned, this time with a few other children.

Once more the girl in white appeared. Bernadette asked the vision to "stay if she came from God, to leave if not." Hedging her bets, Bernadette threw holy water in the direction of the apparition, who merely smiled and inclined her head.

Bernadette's demeanor during the apparition—she was almost deathly pale and immobile throughout—so frightened her companions that they raced to a nearby mill for help. Bernadette's mother, in obvious distress, ran to the grotto from town. Embarrassed by Bernadette's actions, she had to be restrained from beating her daughter.

By the time of the third apparition, on February 18, many in Lourdes were taking a keen interest in Bernadette's tale. Some pressed her to ask the vision who she was. But when Bernadette came to the vision with paper and pen and asked for a name, the vision simply laughed, and spoke for the first time: "Would you have the goodness to come here for fifteen days?"

Bernadette returned, now accompanied by a growing crowd, and the vision continued to appear. After the sixth apparition, on February 21, Bernadette was harshly questioned by the dubious local police commissioner, who tried to ascertain if she was merely pulling a childish prank.

During the investigation, he tried to get her to say that she was seeing the Virgin Mary, but Bernadette persisted in referring to the vision as *aqueró* ("that thing"). When pressed to elaborate, Bernadette described the vision as wearing "a white robe drawn together with a blue sash, a white veil over her head, and a yellow rose on each foot."

Reading the actual police transcripts, one discovers the honesty, simplicity, and persistence in Bernadette that would later impress her supporters. "Stalwart," Ruth Harris calls her.

When the police commissioner was taking notes, he slyly changed the record and read it back to her. "The virgin smiles at me," he said.

"I didn't say *the virgin*," said Bernadette, correcting him.

For me, this is the most compelling aspect of Bernadette Soubirous. She was wholly uninterested in impressing anyone. She avoided saying, until almost the final apparition, that she was seeing the Virgin Mary (though others in the town claimed this almost from the beginning). She was, despite her family's poverty, unwilling to profit in any way from her experiences, refusing any and all gifts. In all her testimonies, Bernadette simply told what she saw and what she didn't see, what she heard and didn't hear.

In this way Bernadette reminds me of her country-woman Joan of Arc. In 1431, during her trial before the ecclesiastical judges who questioned her visions of the saints, Joan responded to their doubts. "I have told you often enough that they are St. Margaret and St. Catherine," she said. "Believe me if you like."

This, in essence, is what Bernadette said, and continues to say: Here is what I have experienced. Believe me if you like.

On February 25, after the seventh and eighth apparitions, Bernadette returned to the grotto. The assembled crowd saw Bernadette not in an ecstatic state, as in previous visits, but clawing at the ground in the grotto, drinking some muddy water that she had uncovered, and stuffing her mouth with weeds.

Bernadette later explained her actions: "She told me. 'Go and drink of the spring and wash yourself in it.' Not seeing any water, I went to the Gave. But she indicated with her finger that I should go under the rock." The eating of the weeds was an act of penance, said Bernadette, for sinners.

But to onlookers Bernadette was merely scratching at the dirt and eating weeds. They were, predictably, horrified. "She's nuts!" someone shouted out. Her aunts, who had accompanied her, gave her a sharp smack as they left the grotto.

In the movie *The Song of Bernadette,* Bernadette's humiliation (Jennifer Jones looks imploringly at the vision with her face covered in mud) leads to the film's dramatic high point. After the protagonist and the crowd leave the grotto, a townsman sits down to rest at the site. As the camera focuses on his hand resting on the dry ground, a few drops, then a trickle, and then a little stream flow past.

"Look at it!" he shouts to swelling music.

In reality, as René Laurentin describes it in *Bernadette of Lourdes,* a small group of townspeople stayed behind to examine the hole Bernadette had begun, and the more they dug, the more pure water gushed forth. But even the movie's account underlines the significance of the day: Bernadette had uncovered the fountain that would become the focus of later pilgrimages and hope for healings.

Again Bernadette was questioned, and annoyed officials redoubled their efforts to frighten her into recanting. Again, she stuck to her story. Two days later, Bernadette returned to the grotto and drank from the spring. On March 1, a local woman whose fall from a tree had left her with a permanently crippled arm went to the spring and plunged her arm in the water. In a few moments her bent fingers straightened and the arm was healed. It would be the first of many miracles attributed to the spring at Lourdes.

Interest over Bernadette's vision continued to mount, and at the thirteenth apparition, Bernadette was accompanied by more than fifteen hundred people. After this apparition she raced to Abbé Peyramale to tell him what the vision had said to her: "Go, tell the priests to come here in procession and build a chapel here." As René Laurentin notes, the priest was appalled, imagining the opprobrium that would descend on him if he were to authorize a ridiculous request from a poor young girl.

So the practical Peyramale demanded some answers from the vision. "Ask her for a name," he said bluntly to Bernadette. "And, as an added test, ask her to make the grotto's wild rosebush flower."

During the next apparition, Bernadette did just that, but the vision merely smiled. No rosebushes bloomed and no name was given. The priest told her again, "If the lady really wishes that a chapel be built, she must tell us her name and make the rosebush bloom."

On March 25, the rosebush was still not in bloom, but a name was given. According to Bernadette, the vision clasped her hands and said, "Que soy era Immaculada Concepciou." Or "I am the Immaculate Conception."

Bernadette, whose religious training was rudimentary at best, had no idea what this meant. She kept repeating the phrase over and over, lest she forget it, as she rushed to Abbé Peyramale.

The film's depiction of her meeting with her pastor corresponds well to what really happened next. Charles Bickford, as Abbé Peyramale, questions Bernadette severely. "The Immaculate Conception. Do you know what that means?" he demands.

Jennifer Jones, as Bernadette, shakes her head.

Her pastor explains (in reality he wrote this in a letter to the bishop) that the name is nonsensical. A few years before, the doctrine of the Immaculate Conception had been proclaimed by the Vatican, holding that the Virgin Mary had been conceived without the stain of original sin. But to say, "I am the Immaculate Conception" was ridiculous, like saying not "I am white," but "I am whiteness." Still, both the Hollywood Bernadette and the real one stuck to their stories.

After this came two more apparitions, and by the time of the final one, the police had boarded up the front of the grotto to prevent any gatherings of the faithful. On July 16, on the Feast of Our Lady of Mount Carmel, Bernadette was forced to view the grotto from across the Gave River. But no matter: "I saw neither the boards nor the Gave," she said. "It seemed to me that I was in the grotto, no more distant than the other times. I saw only the Holy Virgin."

With this final apparition, Bernadette's life changed once again. Greatly admired, hounded by the faithful, and even pressed to perform miracles in her hometown (she resisted, of course), Bernadette became the object of fascination for increasing numbers of pilgrims. In 1860, partially to escape her growing fame and partially to receive more of a formal education, she entered a small convent school in Lourdes.

But her candor and straightforward attitude remained. In 1861, she was photographed for the first time. Urged by the photographer to adopt the precise pose and expression that she had had during the apparitions, Bernadette protested, "But she isn't here."

Five years later, at age twenty-two, Bernadette entered the convent of the Sisters of Charity in Nevers, France, hundreds of miles from Lourdes. Before leaving Lourdes, she paid a last visit to her beloved grotto. "My mission in Lourdes is finished," she said.

Even in the convent, Bernadette was reluctant to discuss her experiences. She told the story of the apparitions only twice to her community, hoping in vain to "hide" herself among her sisters. Always sickly from her childhood asthma, Bernadette was unable to assume many of the tasks of the convent and even found it difficult to pray. "Oh dear," she said, "I don't know how to meditate."

Nonetheless, she was a cheerful person, even in the face of illness, always teasing and laughing with her sisters. In the infirmary one day, she took to embroidery, favoring patterns of small hearts. "If someone tells you that I have no heart," she joked, "tell them I make them all day long."

Gradually she weakened from tuberculosis, and increasingly she was confined to her bed. A cancerous tumor was discovered on her leg, and she declined rapidly. On her deathbed, she returned in her mind to Massabieille. "I have told the events," she told her sister. "Let people abide by what I said the first time. I may have forgotten and so may others. The simpler one writes, the better it will be."

At her death, Bernadette was thirty-five years old.

For most of her life, Bernadette patiently endured endless questions about her visions, consistently refused gifts, and occasionally faced jealousy from some of her sisters in the convent. Always an obedient person, she tried to do her best in a difficult situation but grew weary of repeating the same details to both the faithful and the doubtful.

When one reads her story, with its details of a poor and hungry childhood, constant demands to answer questions about the apparitions, and even a difficult life in the convent, Bernadette seems at peace only when she is in the grotto.

As Ruth Harris writes, "Like the photographs that tried to capture her during the apparitions, Bernadette obeyed, but seemed to leave her heart somewhere else."

3

Lourdes Diary

Several years after the novitiate, when I was doing my theology studies, a professor of church history recommended Ruth Harris's book on Lourdes. Except on Bernadette's feast day, I had hardly thought about her at all since the novitiate, and I remembered her story only dimly. But when I began Harris's book, I was as captivated as I had been when I first saw *The Song of Bernadette.*

Around the same time, I received a phone call from a man in Washington, DC, who had read an article I had written and wanted to take me to lunch. Always happy for a free meal, I agreed to meet him during his next trip to New York. Rob, as it turned out, was not only a dedicated

Catholic, a good father, and an avid reader, but also a knight of Malta.

"Do you know much about the Order of Malta?" he asked me.

Again, my ignorance of Catholic culture came to the fore. I shook my head no, and Rob gave me a précis of the history of the worldwide Catholic charitable organization—officially titled the Sovereign Military Hospitaller Order of St. John of Jerusalem of Rhodes and of Malta—which dates back to at least the eleventh century. The group boasts a colorful history of work in hospices and even military exploits on behalf of pilgrims traveling to the Holy Land. Technically, the august order is a sovereign state: it enjoys diplomatic relationships with other countries and even is afforded "permanent observer" status at the United Nations, much like the Vatican.

Today the international group concentrates not only on fostering the spiritual life of its members, but also on performing a great many charitable works, especially in its support of Catholic hospitals. The order consists of men and women (knights and dames), priests, brothers, bishops, and the occasional cardinal. Among its members are those who, like men and women of other religious orders, pronounce solemn vows to the order. And like other religious orders, it is governed by a superior (in this case called the Grand Master), who lives in the group's headquarters in Rome.

The Order of Malta has a special connection with another location, too.

"One of our biggest works is an annual trip to Lourdes," Rob told me. "We stay for seven days. And it's just an amazing experience. Would you ever think about coming along as a chaplain?"

I told Rob how surprising his offer was: I was right in the middle of Harris's book about Lourdes. But, though flattered, I turned down his kind invitation. "Too busy," I said. Rob smiled and told me that he would persist in asking me until I finally agreed to come.

He kept his promise. The following summer he called me while I was directing a retreat—a time when one naturally feels more open and free—and invited me again in earnest to work as a chaplain on the next trip. And would I like to bring along two other Jesuits to work with me?

"Sure," I said. "Sign us up."

Finding Jesuits was easy: two friends—Brian, a young priest working at a retreat house, and George, a prison chaplain who would be ordained a month after our trip—signed on with alacrity.

As the time approached for our departure, I bought a little spiral-bound notebook to keep as a journal of our pilgrimage to Bernadette's city.

Wednesday, April 28

The Order of Malta has asked us to arrive at Baltimore/Washington International Airport three hours before our 7:00 p.m. charter flight direct to Tarbes-Lourdes-Pyrenees International Airport, which is located a few kilometers from Lourdes. We are greeted by a sea of people, mostly middle-aged or elderly, some wearing silver medals dangling from red ribbons denoting the number of pilgrimages made. Many in the group seem to know one another. Rob makes a beeline for George, Brian, and me and welcomes us to the group.

Scattered in the crowd are men and women seated in wheelchairs or looking painfully thin. Couples cradle children obviously suffering from illness or birth defects. These are, as I already know from Ruth Harris's book, the *malades,* or the sick, the main reason for the journey. Their trips have been paid for by the order—a wonderful act of charity. Everyone, including the *malades,* boards the plane cheerfully.

The flight begins unlike any I've been on, with a bishop leading us in the rosary. The in-flight movie, not surprisingly, is *The Song of Bernadette,* which I have not seen for many years. It corresponds reasonably well to the original story of the apparitions at Lourdes, though it doesn't show enough of Bernadette's natural toughness—which to me makes her a more convincing saint than the film's softer version.

Thursday, April 29

We land after a long flight, and a sleepless one for me. The bus ride from the airport through a rainy countryside studded with tall poplars is full of lively conversation, and we quickly arrive at our lodgings, the Hôtel Saint Sauveur. Seemingly all the hotels and shops at Lourdes have religious names, and it is startling to see a shop selling tacky souvenirs that is named after Charles de Foucauld, who lived in extreme poverty in the desert, or, worse, a knickknack shop under a sign proclaiming *L'Immaculée Conception*.

After lunch, our group (there are perhaps 250 of us) processes to Mass in what will become our usual style: the *malades* seated in small hand-pulled carts in front, accompanied by friends or family, followed by the rest of us.

A letter I received before our departure said, unexpectedly, "Your cassock can be worn anywhere at any time. It will be useful for the Mass in the grotto if the weather is cold, and of course during all the processions." Jesuits haven't worn cassocks since the Second Vatican Council ended in the mid-1960s. But rather than risk giving offense, Brian, George, and I scrounged up some Jesuit cassocks before we left, and we have decided to wear them today.

Far from being an embarrassment, as I had expected, the black cassock feels right in Lourdes. As we cross the square in front of the basilica, I notice brown-robed Franciscans, white-robed Dominicans, and even a black-and-white–robed Trappist. While the plain Roman collar makes me feel priestly, the cassock helps me feel very Jesuit. And the cassock is still recognized here. A few days later, a pilgrim greets us with "Ah, les jésuites!"

After Mass in the ornate basilica, someone suggests a visit to the grotto, which I had assumed was far-off. But the church is built directly atop the rocky outcropping, and when I go around the corner and pass huge racks of tall white candles for sale, I am shocked to come upon it.

Now, under the massive bulk of the gray church is the site familiar from holy cards and reproductions in churches around the world: sinuous gray rocks hover over a plain altar before which stands a huge iron candelabrum. In a small niche, where the apparitions occurred, a statue of the Virgin is surrounded by the words spoken to Bernadette on March 25, 1858: "Que soy era Immaculada Concepciou."

The area before the grotto is marked off by signs requesting silence, and as I approach I am drawn to the obvious peace of the place: serenity seems to radiate from Massabieille. Hundreds of people are gathered before the space—*malades* in their blue carts, a Polish priest with a group of pilgrims praying the rosary, a young backpacker in jeans kneeling on the ground.

Many stand in line to walk through the grotto. Joining them, I run my hand over the smooth wet rock and am astonished to spy the spring uncovered by Bernadette. I am filled with wonder at being here.

As I pass beneath the Virgin's statue, I notice a host of tiny flowering plants of marvelous variety under her feet, and I think of medieval tapestries.

Here at the grotto I am also reminded of the importance of pilgrimage in the spiritual life.

In a brief essay entitled "Pilgrimage," Kevin White, a Jesuit priest, points out that many stories in both the Old and the New Testaments show how believers have often sought God by traveling to a holy site. After the Jewish people had settled in Israel, for example, the holy city of Jerusalem, whose great temple contained the Ark of the Covenant, became a pilgrimage destination for devout Jews. In fact, several of the psalms—120 through 134—were sung by Jewish pilgrims in their long and arduous travels to Jerusalem. "I was glad when they said to me," says Psalm 122, "'Let us go to the house of the LORD!'"

The Gospel of Luke tells us that it was during one of these journeys that the young Jesus was separated from Mary and Joseph. "Now every year," writes Luke, "his parents went to Jerusalem for the festival of the Passover." Later in his life, Jesus would often journey with his disciples to the holy city. In a wonderful aside in his journals, the Trappist monk Thomas Merton describes how his abbot encouraged him to think of these travelers whenever his spirits flagged during the monastery's common prayers.

"He said," wrote Merton in 1948, "I should think of Jesus going up to Jerusalem with all the pilgrims roaring psalms out of their dusty throats."

The disciples were, in so many ways, pilgrims. And, of course, Jesus himself would die in Jerusalem during a time of pilgrimage.

The subsequent history of Christian pilgrimage is extraordinarily rich, dating from the earliest periods of the church. In the first few centuries of the church, Christian pilgrims began visiting the tombs of martyrs to venerate the relics of the saints. Then, starting around the fourth century, journeys to the Holy Land, where the devout would visit shrines associated with the life of Christ, also became popular.

The Middle Ages was the golden age of pilgrimage, with believers traveling to the Holy Land, to local shrines, and to ones more far-flung. The shrine of Santiago de Compostela, located in Galicia, Spain, is said to be the resting place of the relics of St. James the Great, who is supposed to have traveled to Spain to evangelize the region. The great cathedral there became a major focus for pilgrims in the Middle Ages. Today millions of believers still stream to places like Jerusalem, Rome, and Santiago de Compostela, as well as the Marian shrines scattered across the world, including Lourdes.

Pilgrimages are time-honored ways of fostering reliance on God, so dependent are pilgrims on the grace of God, which manifests itself in the charity and kindness of fellow pilgrims and in those we meet along the way. The time of travel is also what one of my spiritual directors called a liminal time—a transitional moment, or an in-between space. We find ourselves caught between one place and another, and during these times we can be especially aware of God. Removed from our comfortable routines, we are naturally more aware of our fundamental reliance on God, and are therefore often more open to grace.

We are sometimes more attentive to God when our normal routines are set aside, and when our defenses are down.

It is then that we more easily recognize our own "spiritual poverty," that is, our basic need for God.

As the German theologian Johannes Baptist Metz wrote in his book *Poverty of Spirit:* "When the mask falls and the core of our Being is revealed, it soon becomes obvious that we are religious 'by nature,' that religion is the secret dowry of our Being."

Pilgrimages are times when the mask often falls.

Pilgrimages are also an important part of Jesuit training. All Jesuit novices, since the time of St. Ignatius of Loyola in the sixteenth century, have been asked to undertake some kind of pilgrimage as part of their training. It is a way to increase our reliance on God and, not incidentally, remind us that we could live on very little, in terms of possessions. (Sometimes when one travels, one thinks, *I like living so simply!*) My own novitiate pilgrimage was an extended one to the developing country of Jamaica, where I worked with the sick and the poor in a hospice run by the Missionaries of Charity, the religious order founded by Mother Teresa.

Significantly, in his autobiography, St. Ignatius of Loyola refers to himself not as Ignatius, or even by his birth name of Iñigo, but as "the pilgrim."

Yet there are a variety of reasons for taking a pilgrimage. For many who travel to Lourdes, the motivation is to request a special kind of healing, whether physical, emotional, or spiritual. For others, it may be a desire to find some direction or guidance, to express gratitude for some blessing one has received, or even to make amends for some sin in one's life. The intentions dwelling in the souls of the millions who make their way to shrines worldwide are as varied as the pilgrims themselves.

Indeed, the whole of human life can be seen as a pilgrimage to God. For some philosophers in the early church, who understood existence as flowing from God and returning to God, the great journey of life was always directed to our original source. "O Lord," wrote St. Augustine, "our hearts are restless until they rest in you."

This restless journey, this lifelong pilgrimage, reaches its fulfillment in God. The smaller trips we make along the way are reminders of this lifelong journey to the Lord. Or, as St. Catherine of Siena said, "All the way to heaven is heaven."

Dog-tired after dinner, I wander over to the grotto. Purchasing two candles, I pray for my family and place the candles among a mass of others huddled under a metal shed whose wall is engraved with the legend "This flame continues my prayer." My mother has asked for "joy, peace, and strength." And my sister and brother-in-law pray to be able to conceive a child. (Their prayer was answered within six months, and my mother seemed a little more joyful when I returned.)

Nearby, I notice a large group congregating in time for the evening rosary procession. Shortly, thousands of people light their small candles and begin walking together as an announcer declaims the prayers and mysteries of the rosary in French, English, Spanish, Italian, Polish, and German. Each of us carries a slim taper whose flame is surrounded by a white paper lantern, protecting it from the wind. Printed on the lantern are the words to a variety of Marian hymns.

We slowly process around the huge oval pavement before the basilica. After the first decade of the rosary, the crowd begins to sing the "Lourdes Hymn." The crowd's song seems to give voice to my own love for Mary, and it moves me deeply to be in the midst of this wonderful assembly.

As the first "Ave Maria" is sung out over the square, tens of thousands of pilgrims lift their orange-flamed candles in unison, and I am overcome by the sight of this profession of faith: the *malades* and the able-bodied, of all ages, from across the world. It seems a vision of what the world could be.

Late at night I finally get to bed, after almost thirty-six hours awake. I'm sharing a room with Brian, who, I discover upon entering the room, is a champion snorer. His bed is a foot away from my own. After an hour of being unable to sleep, I pull on my cassock and pad downstairs to the hotel lobby, where I reread a bit of Ruth Harris's book *Lourdes.* In another hour, I return to the room, where Brian's snoring has increased in volume.

I lie in bed for a few hours trying to arrive at some spiritual interpretation of the situation. Maybe this is part of a spiritual discipline that God is asking me to accept on pilgrimage. I say a rosary. I think of all the sick and disabled with us, who put up with much worse. And I recall Ruth Harris's comment that the journey to Lourdes for most pilgrims in the early twentieth century was "harrowing." I say another rosary. Then I decide I probably won't do anyone any good as a chaplain if I'm walking around like a zombie.

So, exhausted, I walk downstairs to ask if there are any single rooms available. "Non," says the night clerk with a Gallic shrug. "Pas de chambres, mon père." No rooms.

Hoping for a modicum of rest, I leave the hotel in search of another one. Fortunately, there must be ten hotels on our block. It's about four in the morning, and a fine rain comes down in Lourdes, making the streets slick. Almost comatose now, I spot the Hôtel Moderne across the street and begin walking into the lobby, which, oddly, appears to be open to the night air, and then . . .

Wham!

I walk head-on into a plate-glass window that remained invisible in the darkness. The night clerk rushes to open the door. Disoriented, I blurt out something in French about a room and how much. The desk clerk fixes me with a baleful stare, and I suddenly see myself from his vantage point. Doubtless it looks as if I have returned from a long night of partying on the town. In a cassock!

Squinting at me, he suggests the hotel across the street and swiftly ushers me out the door.

It's almost dawn, so I decide to wait until tomorrow, and I say a prayer to St. Bernadette to find me some new lodgings. Rubbing the bump on my forehead, I return to our room, where Brian snores contentedly. At dawn I walk over to another hotel and find an inexpensive room.

After thanking Bernadette, I take a long nap.

Friday, April 30

A few hours later, I cross the street to my former hotel for a huge breakfast with George and Brian. As I walk over, the night clerk at the Hôtel Moderne spies me through the plate-glass window. He smiles slyly and playfully waggles his finger at me as if to say, "I know all about your revelry last night, Father."

By now, Brian, George, and I have met many members of the order, as well as many of the *malades*. The term is not pejorative here. "We're all *malades* in one way or another," says a bishop on pilgrimage with us. The range of illnesses they live with is stunning: cancer, AIDS, Lyme disease, dementia, birth defects.

At lunch I sit with a couple from Philadelphia. She suffers from a disease I have never heard of, and that has left her, in her late thirties, unable to walk easily and prone to a host of painful physical ailments.

She and her husband are aware of the seriousness of her condition, but they are consistently friendly, happy, and solicitous, and I like them immediately. "Oh, I'm *fine*," she says. "I've been laughing since I got here. So many funny things have happened!" As we process to Mass, Brian and George quietly explain the conditions faced by other *malades* they have met.

Lourdes, of course, is famous for its healing waters, though nothing in the words of Mary to Bernadette suggests that the waters can heal. (She merely said, "Go drink of the waters and bathe yourself there.") The short guide we receive from the Order of Malta wisely counsels against expecting physical healings. Spiritual healing is more common for pilgrims. But I pray for actual physical healing for the *malades* anyway, especially the ones I know, here and at home.

In the afternoon, our group goes to the stations of the cross, located on the side of a steep hill. The life-size figures are painted a lurid gold. The knights and dames of the order assist many of the *malades* along the rocky terrain in a cold drizzle. We are handed a small booklet called *Everyone's Way of the Cross,* and I groan inwardly, expecting banal sentiments.

But I am wrong. If the writing is simple, the prayers are powerful, particularly as I notice a frail man being helped over the slippery ground by his companion.

"Lord, I know what you are telling me," says the text for the fourth station. "To watch the pain of those we love is harder than to bear our own."

The afternoon is a good chance to spend some time in prayer at the grotto, even in the chilly rain. In the weeks before my departure, I started asking friends and family members if they had any intentions that they might like me to remember at Lourdes. I was astonished by the response. Even my agnostic friends had heard of Lourdes and asked for prayers. The requests grew so numerous that I began to write them down on a little note card, to guard against forgetting anyone's intentions. (And almost everyone, no matter what his or her beliefs, asked if I could bring back some Lourdes water.)

Now I take from my wallet that folded note card covered with almost fifty prayer requests: for the conception of a child from a childless couple, for the remission of cancer from a friend's sister, for good luck in finding a job from another friend. As I stand under an umbrella, I imagine myself standing before Mary and Bernadette, presenting each petitioner to them and asking them to bring our prayers to God. It takes almost an hour to go through the list, but when I am finished I feel as if I have completed an important assignment.

Tonight's rosary procession is, if possible, as moving as last night's. Somehow, in the midst of this huge crowd, Brian, George, and I are spotted by one of the officials of the Domaine, that is, the sprawling area surrounding the grotto and the basilica. "Vous êtes prêtres?" he asks. "Are you priests?" When I nod, he pulls us through the crowd to the steps of the basilica. There we join other priests, who gaze out at the enormous throng, just then raising their voices in the "Lourdes Hymn" in the damp night air. An English priest turns to me and says, "The universal church looks well tonight, doesn't it?"

Saturday, May 1

This morning I am waiting for a turn at the baths. On long wooden benches under a stone portico sit the *malades,* along with their companions and other pilgrims. Flanking me are two men from our pilgrimage with the Order of Malta. One, a fortyish red-haired man, is strangely quiet: later I learn that he is suffering from a form of dementia brought on by Lyme disease. His caring wife suffers greatly. Carved in the stone wall are the Virgin's words to Bernadette: "Go drink of the waters and bathe yourself there." Every few minutes an "Ave Maria" is sung in another language.

After an hour, the three of us are called into a small room surrounded by blue and white striped curtains. Once inside we strip to our undershorts and wait patiently on plastic chairs. From the other side of another curtain I hear the splashing of someone entering the bath, and in a few seconds he emerges with a wide grin.

As I wonder if the legend that Lourdes water dries off "miraculously" is true, another curtain parts. A smiling attendant invites me inside: "Mon père, s'il vous plaît."

Inside a small chamber three men stand around a sunken stone bath. My high school French comes in handy and we chat amiably. One volunteer points to a wooden peg, and after I hang up my undershorts, he quickly wraps a cold wet towel around my waist. ("I think they kept it in the freezer for us!" says one of the *malades* at lunch.)

Another volunteer carefully guides me to the lip of the bath and asks me to pray for the healing I need. When I cross myself, they bow their heads and pray along with me. Two of them gently take my arms and lead me down the steps into the bath, where the water is cold, but no colder than a swimming pool.

"Asseyez-vous," one says, and I sit down as they hold my arms. Here, praying in this dimly lit room, in this spring water, held by two kind people, I feel entirely separated from the rest of my life. It's a kind of mini-retreat, removed from the rest of the world but somehow very much part of it.

And then—*whoosh*—they stand me up and point to a small statue of Mary, whose feet I kiss. Then I'm handed a quick drink of water from a pitcher.

As I emerge from the bath, a volunteer asks me to bless him and the others. Wearing only a towel, I bless the men, who kneel on the wet stone floor and cross themselves. "The first time you've blessed without your clothes?" asks one, and we laugh.

After the bath, I rush over to the Grotto of Massabieille, where our group is celebrating Mass. And, yes, the water dries from my skin immediately.

At the end of the Mass, the presider asks the congregation to pass up any petitions that we have brought. I'm happy that I still have my little note card full of prayer requests in my wallet, and I hand it to a man collecting scraps of paper and envelopes from people in the crowd. The pieces of paper are all stuffed in a small gray box that stands near the spring in the grotto, and I briefly wonder how God will be able to sort them all out, but I trust that God will, somehow.

At five o'clock, Brian and I walk through a light drizzle to a nearby Carmelite monastery. The plain white chapel, with low wooden benches for pews and a carved Crucifixion scene on the sanctuary wall, is utterly quiet and a welcome break from the crowds. We sit for a few minutes until a bell rings loudly. A dozen nuns silently file in for Vespers. They sit behind a tall iron grate to the left side of the altar, separating them from the rest of the chapel.

Seeing their brown and white habits reminds me of the nineteenth-century French saint Thérèse of Lisieux, whose own Carmelite community is located in the north of the country. Thérèse is one of my favorite saints. Raised in a tight-knit family, almost smothered with affection by her father and her sisters, Thérèse entered a Carmelite convent in the town of Lisieux at the age of fifteen. Protesting that in the garden of life, she could never hope to be a great rose or an impressive lily, she instead decided to be content as a "little flower," concentrating on doing small things with great love. Thérèse believed that God blesses each of us individually:

> Just as the sun shines simultaneously on the tall cedars and on each little flower as though it were alone on the earth, so Our Lord is occupied particularly with each soul, as though there were no others. And just as in nature all the seasons are arranged in such a way as to make the humblest daisy bloom on a set day, in the same way, everything works out for the good of each soul.

This spirituality, often called the Little Way, is most clearly described in her famous autobiography, *The Story of a Soul,* published shortly after her death, in 1897, at age twenty-four.

The chanting of the Carmelite sisters is beautiful—done in high, clear, girlish voices—and it dawns on me that their songs are probably close to the words and tunes that Thérèse heard each day of her life in the monastery at Lisieux. As plainchant fills the chapel, I feel very near to Thérèse and overwhelmed with a sense of the holiness of her life, and I find myself filled with emotion.

Sunday, May 2

A gargantuan church, called the Basilica of St. Pius X, was built underground in 1958 near the Grotto of Massabieille. It seats, unbelievably, twenty thousand people. The concrete structure would resemble an enormous oval parking lot were it not for the huge portraits of saints, perhaps ten feet high, that line the walls. One banner, portraying Pope John XXIII, reads "Bienheureux Jean XXIII." The French word for "blessed" means, literally, "well-happy" and seems a far better one than our own. In the morning our group processes to the underground church for a solemn Mass for the Order of Malta.

There are scores of priests in the sacristy, dozens of bishops, and even three cardinals. The entrance procession, with tens of thousands of *malades,* their companions, knights, dames, pilgrims, students, and everybody else, is almost alarmingly joyful. High above the floor, mammoth screens show the words of the verses of the "Lourdes Hymn," which, now in English, now in French, now in Italian, now in Spanish, now in German, is taken up by the throng.

At communion I am handed a gold ciborium brimming with Hosts and am pointed to a young Italian guard who carries a yellow flag. He has a girlfriend in America, he explains, and maybe she could call me if she needs to talk? With his flag aloft, he leads me into a sea of people, who engulf me and reach their hands out for communion as if it's the most important thing in the world. Which, of course, it is.

Later on, as I am walking in front of the basilica with a Franciscan friend, a French pilgrim asks me to hear a confession. We sit on a stone bench in the sun, and when we have finished, I look up. A little line has formed, and I call my Franciscan friend over to help.

An Italian man sits down next to me. "Italiano?" he says, and I nod. But my Italian is very poor, and after a few minutes I am utterly lost. Before giving him absolution, I tell him that while I might not have understood everything he has said, God has.

In the afternoon I wander through town searching for little gifts for friends at home. Before I left the States I heard some Jesuits lament the tackiness of the shops here, but

I'm not bothered by them. Most shoppers, I imagine, are thinking of people at home, and so buying souvenirs is just another way of remembering people while at Lourdes.

Looking at a rack of rosary beads, I see an exact copy of the rosary I bought twenty years ago at the Cathedral of Notre Dame in Paris, right after graduating from college.

The rosary is everywhere in Lourdes. It is present not simply during the grand rosary processions in the evenings, but in quieter ways as well. You see people kneeling on the cold stone ground of the grotto and fingering the beads of their rosaries, wandering around the Domaine with them clutched behind their backs, and even furtively taking them from their pockets in the hotels to pass what little free time they have in prayer.

Whenever I see the pilgrims with their rosaries, I wonder when they first received them. Perhaps their mother and father gave them their rosary on the day of their first Holy Communion, as my parents did for me. Perhaps the rosary was a gift from a beloved aunt or uncle or priest or sister. Or perhaps they purchased their rosary themselves at another Marian shrine far from here: at Fátima, in Portugal; or Knock, in Ireland; or Medjugorje, in Bosnia and Herzegovina.

The rosary that I'm looking at in the little souvenir shop has a tiny metal disk attached to the chain with a portrait of Mary on one side and the word *indécrochable* on the other. When I returned from Paris all those years ago, I looked up the word in a French-English dictionary, which defined it as "strong or unable to be defiled." And I thought that was a good title to apply to Mary: *Indécrochable.*

The shopkeeper comes over. "Ah oui," says madame. "C'est indécrochable." Then in English she says, "That means these beads are unbreakable." She gives them a tug. "See how strong they are?"

I laugh and tell her that I thought the word applied to Mary, not to the beads. That it was sort of a theological title—*Immaculée, Indécrochable.* The shopkeeper laughs heartily and quickly tells her assistant, who smiles indulgently. "No," the shopkeeper says in English. "This is not a theological title. This is a marketing title!"

Monday, May 3

At six-thirty this morning, some thirty of us leave in a tour bus for the house of Bernadette Soubirous. On the way over, we pass dozens of souvenir shops, and George leans over to me. "Bernadette was lucky, wasn't she?" he whispers. "On the way back from the grotto she could stop off and buy some souvenirs for herself." Two women, *malades,* sitting in front of us hear his comment and giggle.

Bernadette's small house, the *cachot,* is located on a narrow side street. Astonishingly, it is even smaller than the horrible room depicted in *The Song of Bernadette.* In René Laurentin's biography *Bernadette of Lourdes,* he notes that in this dank hovel, two beds served six people.

Here is Laurentin's description of how Bernadette's family ended up in this hidden place:

At the start of 1857, the Soubirous family were thrown on to the street again, [thanks to] continuing unemployment. They were forced to quit their seedy lodging in the Rives house, leaving behind their wardrobe in pawn to the proprietor. Moving was becoming easier and easier, since their load was lighter each time. Where were they to find a roof over their heads? Where were they to find an even worse place to take them in? No one wanted the Soubirouses anymore. The last chance open to them was the Jail, which was described as a "foul, somber hovel" by Prosecutor Dutour in his report of March 1, 1858.

Before we arrived, a sister arranged the *cachot* for Mass, which will be celebrated by Theodore Cardinal McCarrick, archbishop of Washington, DC, who has joined our group for a few days. Because of the room's size, only the *malades* and their companions can fit, along with the cardinal, another priest, and us, the three Jesuits: two of us priests and one a deacon.

As the Mass begins, I see thirty people, many of them seriously ill, turn their expectant faces to the cardinal. He puts them at ease instantly, saying that we all feel like sardines, and not to worry about standing up during the Mass, since sardines don't have to. Everyone laughs.

Yesterday the cardinal led a huge Eucharistic procession near the grotto; it is a marvel to see a priest who can preach both to thousands and to a handful of people. He offers a short, moving homily on the meaning of suffering. "God loves us," he says. "God wants to be with us in our suffering.

And God tries to give us hope in our suffering through the person of Jesus Christ."

I think of the incongruity of it all: we are here because of a poor fourteen-year-old girl who came from the simplest of backgrounds and then returned to her hidden life. Robert Ellsberg remarks on this in his book *Blessed among All Women*:

> In traditional stories of the saints it is common to remark on the many ways, even as children, that they stood out among their neighbors. But even the most zealous admirers of St. Bernadette, try as they might, could find little to distinguish her. She was good, honest, and devout; on this much everyone agrees. Otherwise she was quite ordinary. She considered herself of no importance, simply a poor vehicle of God's grace, who was content to withdraw into obscurity once her mission was complete.

During the rainy afternoon I spend a few hours in a vaguely Gothic building with a white and blue sign out front that reads "Confessions." In front of the building is a stone statue of a kneeling St. John Vianney, the nineteenth-century French priest known for his compassion in the confessional. It was said that St. John, known as the Curé d'Ars, or the curate of Ars, spent upwards of eighteen hours a day hearing confessions.

In a narrow hallway, people sit placidly on benches outside doors that announce confessions in English, Spanish, French, Dutch, German, and Italian. There seem to be far more Germans than anyone else. Every few minutes someone pops into my English cubicle and asks hopefully, "Deutsch?"

Tuesday, May 4

Tomorrow we will return to the States, so I decide to return to the baths today. By now I have gotten to know a few of the attendants who help the pilgrims seated on the benches under the stone portico. I ask one how he likes his job. "Oh, it's not a job!" he says cheerfully. "I'm a volunteer, like everyone else here! If it were just a job, then I would be thinking, *One euro for each person I help.* Or, maybe, *One euro for each kilo that the person weighs!*" He laughs. "But this way I look at everybody like a person, not a number."

He says that many pilgrims are nervous and worried when they come for the first time. "C'est naturel," he says. "People might be sick, or they might be cold, or they might be afraid of slipping inside." But his first experience, he says, was transforming. He struggles to find the words in English and then switches back to French. "I felt as if a door had opened in my heart." He flings his hands away from his chest to demonstrate. "After that, nothing was the same."

Once inside, I see a gregarious attendant I have met before, and with a broad smile he shouts out, "Mon ami!" The other volunteer notices my cassock and says, "You are a Jesuit? Then you know my family." When I look confused, he says, "I am Polish and my name is Kostka." So I am helped into the bath by *mon ami* and a member of the family of St. Stanislaus Kostka, one of my Jesuit heroes.

In the afternoon, after filling a few plastic bottles with water from the taps near the grotto, I return to my hotel. Brushing my teeth in my bathroom, I think that if Mary were to appear today, it would probably be in a place as unlikely as a bathroom. After all, the original apparitions occurred at Massabieille, a filthy place where pigs came to forage.

A few minutes later, when I enter the hotel lobby, an elderly man from our group asks to speak with me about something that happened to him in the baths this morning.

This rational and sensible Catholic has come to Lourdes after a long illness. (I've changed some of the details here, but not the essentials.) Through tears, he says that after the bath, he was in the men's bathroom and heard a woman's voice say in a few words that his sins were forgiven. The bathroom was entirely empty, and there are, obviously, no women anywhere near the men's baths at Lourdes.

Before coming to Lourdes, he had prayed for this grace: despite a recent confession he still felt the weight of his sins. In response, I tell him that God communicates with us in many ways, and that while people rarely report this type of experience, it is not unheard of. Something similar represented a pivotal event in Mother Teresa's life.

He is surprised when I tell him that I was just thinking that a bathroom wouldn't be such a bad place for a religious experience. And though his experience was unexpected, it makes sense: a grace received in a clear and distinct way while on pilgrimage. Besides, I say, your sins really are forgiven.

"What did the voice sound like?" I ask. "Oh," he says. "Very peaceful."

Our conversation reminds me that God can communicate with us in any way God wishes to. Most of us will probably never experience God's communication the same way that my friend did in that little bathroom in Lourdes.

But there are other, no less important ways that God can communicate with us. God can speak to us through our emotions—in the happiness we feel for a bit of good news, in the love we feel for our family and friends, in the awe we feel before a beautiful sunset, in the gratitude we feel during "peak" events in our lives, like the birth of a child. God can speak to us through other people in our lives—a spouse or family member, a friend or coworker, even a homeless person we meet on the street. God can speak to us through the Scriptures, as we are able to connect a particular passage or story with our own experience. God can speak to us in our prayer, as we gain insight into the life of Christ and the invitation that God offers to anyone seeking meaning in life.

In essence, God speaks to us in as many ways as there are believers. The key is being aware and attentive enough to recognize this.

Tonight the Order of Malta hosts a farewell dinner for everyone, full of speeches, songs, a few hastily arranged skits, and some jokey awards. I win an award for valorous service (in light of my blessing people without the benefit of clothes). My friend Brian, as I know, is not only a Jesuit priest but also an Irish step dancer, and when he begins his spirited high-stepping the room erupts in laughter and applause. "Can all Jesuits do that?" someone at my table asks over the cheers.

The youngest *malades,* children with scoliosis, cancer, and birth defects, sing a little song, hesitant and off-key, that leaves many in the crowd near tears.

Later that night one of the knights tells me that the boy with scoliosis, one of the most cheerful children one could ever hope to meet, said that his classmates might be sad when he returns to school. "They thought that I would be tall and that my back would be straight," he explained. He had visited the baths just this morning, with no apparent physical change.

"But that's okay," he said. "I'll be tall and my back will be straight in heaven."

The story recounted by Bernadette Soubirous is difficult for even some devout Catholics to accept. Of course, it's not essential that a Catholic believe in this story or in the apparitions at Lourdes, as one needs to believe in, say, the Resurrection. And the church's tradition on this is clear, as explained in the *Catechism of the Catholic Church,* in a passage on "private" revelations.

> Throughout the ages, there have been so-called "private" revelations, some of which have been recognized by the authority of the Church. They do not belong, however, to the deposit of faith. It is not their role to improve or complete Christ's definitive Revelation, but to help live more fully by it in a certain period of history. Guided by the Magisterium of the Church, the *sensus fidelium* [sense of the faithful] knows how to discern and

welcome in these revelations whatever constitutes an authentic call of Christ or his saints to the Church.

The Virgin's message was simple and sensible: penance, prayer, pilgrimage. And it is this, not simply the many well-attested healings at Lourdes over the years, that has made Bernadette's visions one of the few private revelations officially accepted by the Catholic Church.

Still, many have their doubts.

But the natural beauty of the story and Bernadette's personal character have made it easy for me to accept. I am reminded of a passage from one of my favorite novels, *Brideshead Revisited,* by the English novelist Evelyn Waugh. Early in the book, set in 1920s England, a young Catholic named Sebastian is being pestered by the narrator over his belief in the story of the birth of Jesus, as recounted in the Bible. The narrator is also mocking his friend for his belief in Catholicism in general:

"But, my dear Sebastian, you can't seriously *believe* it all."

"Can't I?"

"I mean about Christmas and the star and the three kings and the ox and the ass."

"Oh yes, I believe that. It's a lovely idea."

"But you can't *believe* things because they're a lovely idea."

"But I *do*. That's how I believe."

Of course, even before traveling to Lourdes, I knew that Bernadette's tale was much more than just a lovely idea. And somehow, after visiting Lourdes, I have become even more convinced of the truth of her story, thanks to the place itself and the people I have met here.

Early on my last morning here, before our flight, I make a final visit to the grotto. Even before dawn, a Mass is being celebrated, and pilgrims are already here, kneeling before the space, running their hands over the rock, praying the rosary, and hoping for healing, as they have been since 1858.

The sun rises over the basilica, and the bells chime the first clear notes of the "Lourdes Hymn" as I cross the square.

4

The Grotto of Our Hearts

I returned to Lourdes the following year. "You're on our list now!" Rob had said cheerfully at the end of our first trip. And I wondered if my second trip to Lourdes would be as intense as my first one. After all, the first one had been a profound experience: I felt powerful emotions on many occasions during the seven days I spent in the town.

My second visit, as it turned out, was different. (For one thing, it was sunnier. Rather than worrying about catching a cold, I worried about sunburn!) And while George was delighted to accompany me again, our friend Brian wasn't able to: he was working with the Jesuits in Myanmar (formerly Burma), teaching in a seminary there. George and

I promised to pray for our missionary friend during our return trip to the grotto.

"Which of you will be doing the Irish dancing this year?" one of the knights asked us on the flight. George and I pointed at each other and said in unison, "*He* will!"

Since I was already familiar with the main attractions of the shrine—the dark, brooding church; the nighttime candlelit processions; and even the Carmelite monastery outside the walls of the Domaine—this year I could spend more time with the *malades* and their companions, hearing their struggles, listening to their hopes, and, sometimes, just laughing with them.

And this year, on a sort of break day, George and I paid a visit to Loyola, the birthplace of the founder of the Jesuits, located just across the border in Spain. It was a wonderful trip in which everything seemed to happen at just the right time: we arrived at the great basilica in the center of town just in time for Mass, we stumbled on a small chapel in the ancestral home of St. Ignatius of Loyola just in time for a second Mass, we ran into a Jesuit brother just in time for lunch at the Jesuit community, and we returned home just in time for dinner at our hotel in Lourdes.

Sometimes in life, when it seems like nothing is going right, I think about St. Catherine of Siena's statement "Nothing great is ever achieved without much enduring." But during our trip to Loyola, I thought of St. Paul's observation that "all things work together for good for those who love God."

When I returned to our hotel in Lourdes, I ran into a young volunteer with the Order of Malta and told her how perfectly everything seemed to work out on our little excursion to Loyola.

"It's like a confirmation of your vocation as a Jesuit!" she said. I had to agree.

But there was one thing that was very much the same on my second trip to Lourdes: the grotto, perhaps the most prayerful place I've ever experienced. Each time I went to the grotto, I found myself able to pray. Perhaps the reason is that there are always dozens of pilgrims praying at the place, around the clock. Perhaps it is the uncanny formation of the rocks there, which seems physically to draw you in, as if God is pulling you near. Most likely, it is the fact that Mary's appearances there in 1858 have blessed the place, making it a natural spot for contemplation and reflection. I spent even more time praying than I had during my first trip.

Lourdes is now one of those places where I have met God in a special way. The building that housed my Jesuit novitiate is one such place. A retreat house located on a windswept promontory in Gloucester, Massachusetts, on the Atlantic coastline, is another. So is the church at the Abbey of Gethsemani, tucked away in the hills of rural Kentucky outside Louisville, where my great hero Thomas Merton lived.

For some, these sites may seem like any other building or locale. Unlike the grotto at Lourdes, they were not the sites of anything miraculous. But for me these places have become outward signs of God's grace, places that are almost sacramental. William Wordsworth, in his poem *The Prelude*, called these places "spots of time," retaining memories of those events that are so potent that simply recalling them enables our souls to be "nourished and invisibly repaired."

Perhaps you are reading this and thinking: *I remember my own trip to Lourdes.*

Or maybe you are thinking: *I hope someday to go to Lourdes.*

Just as likely you are thinking, maybe even with some sadness or disappointment, *I may never be able to go to Lourdes*—because of illness or financial constraints or lack of time. But it's good to remember that God gives us the ability to pray deeply wherever we are. While Mary appeared to Bernadette in a specific locale, and at a specific time, the Spirit is with us always and everywhere.

We need not travel to southern France to encounter God's presence in our lives. God dwells within us already, and just as important as the grotto of Lourdes, where Mary spoke in 1858, is the grotto of our hearts, where God speaks to us every day.

There is no lack of excellent resources about Lourdes and St. Bernadette. Perhaps the best and most scholarly is Ruth Harris's exhaustive look at the history of the site, *Lourdes: Body and Spirit in the Secular Age.* Harris, an Oxford historian, is a self-described agnostic, but she takes a sympathetic approach to the happenings at Lourdes and takes Bernadette at her word. A more overtly Catholic but no less scholarly presentation of the events is René Laurentin's *Bernadette of Lourdes: A Life Based on Authenticated Documents.* Fr. Laurentin, a Benedictine priest and historian, offers about as detailed an account of the apparitions and the life of Bernadette as you will find. Finally, Franz Werfel's novel *The Song of Bernadette,* the book that introduced Bernadette to millions (and inspired the popular film), sticks close to the facts and also makes for a terrific read.

In fact, the story of Franz Werfel's book itself would make a good book. Fleeing the Nazis who had overrun France in 1940, the Austrian author Werfel and his wife found refuge in the town of Lourdes, and he was deeply moved by the story of Bernadette Soubirous and what happened to her in 1858. One day Werfel made a vow that if he ever reached America he would write Bernadette's story. "This book," he writes in the preface, "is the fulfillment of my vow."

✧BIBLIOGRAPHY✧

Butler, Alban. *Butler's Lives of the Saints*, rev. ed. Edited by Michael Walsh. San Francisco: HarperSanFrancisco, 1991.

Catechism of the Catholic Church. 2nd ed. Vatican City: Libreria Editrice Vaticana, 1997.

Cunningham, Lawrence S. *A Brief History of Saints*. Oxford: Blackwell, 2005.

Ellsberg, Robert. *Blessed among All Women: Women Saints, Prophets, and Witnesses for Our Time*. New York: Crossroad, 2005.

Enzler, Clarence. *Everyone's Way of the Cross*. Notre Dame, IN: Ave Maria Press, 2002.

Harris, Ruth. *Lourdes: Body and Spirit in the Secular Age*. New York: Viking, 1999.

Joan of Arc. *Joan of Arc: In Her Own Words*. Translated by Willard Trask. New York: Turtle Point Press, 1996.

Johnson, Elizabeth A. *Friends of God and Prophets: A Feminist Theological Reading of the Communion of Saints*. New York: Continuum, 1998.

Laurentin, René. *Bernadette of Lourdes: A Life Based on Authenticated Documents.* Translated by John Drury. London: Darton, Longman and Todd, 1979.

McBrien, Richard P. *The HarperCollins Encyclopedia of Catholicism.* New York: HarperCollins, 1995.

Merton, Thomas. *New Seeds of Contemplation.* Norfolk, CT: New Directions, 1972.

———. *The Sign of Jonas.* New York: Harcourt Brace Jovanovich, 1979.

Metz, Johannes Baptist. *Poverty of Spirit.* Translated by John Drury. New York: Paulist Press, 1998.

Phan, Peter C., ed. *The Directory on Popular Piety and the Liturgy: Principles and Guidelines: A Commentary.* Collegeville, MN: Liturgical Press, 2005.

Waugh, Evelyn. *Brideshead Revisited.* New York: Alfred A. Knopf, 1993.

Werfel, Franz. *The Song of Bernadette.* Translated by Ludwig Lewisohn. New York: St. Martin's, 1989.

White, Kevin. "Pilgrimage." In *Awake My Soul: Contemporary Catholics on Traditional Devotions,* edited by James Martin. Chicago: Loyola Press, 2004.

ABOUT THE AUTHOR

James Martin, SJ, is a Jesuit priest and associate editor of *America,* a national Catholic magazine. A graduate of the University of Pennsylvania's Wharton School of Business, he worked for six years in corporate finance before entering the Society of Jesus in 1988. During his Jesuit training he worked in a hospice in Kingston, Jamaica; with street-gang members in Chicago; as a prison chaplain in Boston; and for two years with East African refugees in Nairobi, Kenya. After completing his philosophy and theology studies, he was ordained a priest in 1999.

Fr. Martin's writing has appeared in a variety of newspapers and magazines, and he is a frequent commentator in the media on religion. He is the author or editor of a number of books on religion and spirituality, including his memoirs *In Good Company: The Fast Track from the Corporate World to Poverty, Chastity, and Obedience* (Sheed & Ward, 2000) and *This Our Exile: A Spiritual Journey with the Refugees of East Africa* (Orbis, 1999). His most recent book is *My Life with the Saints* (Loyola, 2006).

Returning home from Lourdes on their first visit with the Order of Malta are: seated, left to right, Brian Frain, SJ, and the author, James Martin, SJ; standing, George Williams, SJ. Photograph courtesy of James Martin, SJ.